DISTRICT OF COLUMBIA FLAG

IT'S AMAZING!
MONSTERS

Annabel Savery

A+

Smart Apple Media

Published by Smart Apple Media, an imprint of Black Rabbit Books
P.O. Box 3263, Mankato, Minnesota 56002
www.blackrabbitbooks.com

Printed in the United States of America at Corporate Graphics, North Mankato, Minnesota.

Published by arrangement with the Watts Publishing Group LTD, London.

Library of Congress Cataloging-in-Publication Data
Savery, Annabel.
Monsters / Annabel Savery.
p. cm.—(It's amazing!)
Includes bibliographical references and index.
Summary: "Describes monsters of all kinds from folklore to modern movies, including Greek
Hydras, Norwegian krakens, vampires, and ogres. Also describes real-life monsters such as
sharks and komodo dragons"—Provided by publisher.
ISBN 978-1-59920-689-9 (library binding)
1. Monsters—Juvenile literature. 2. Monsters—Folklore. I. Title.
GR825.S28 2013
001.944—dc23
                      2011025815

Planning and production by Discovery Books Limited
Managing editor: Laura Durman
Editor: Annabel Savery
Designer: Ian Winton

Picture credits: Bigstock.com: p. 21 top (Astoreth), p. 21 bottom (AlienCat); Fortean
Picture Library: p. 19; Getty Images: p. 7 bottom (Bridgeman Art Library), p. 26 (Keystone/
Stringer), p. 29 top (Jon Berkeley/Ikon Images); Istockphoto: p. 6 bottom (Grafissimo),
p. 7 top (Andyworks), p. 14 (Denzorr); Photoshot: p. 16 bottom, p. 18, p. 22, p. 23, p. 24,
p. 25 top, p. 25 bottom; Shutterstock: title & p. 12 (DWL-Designs), p. 4 (Linda Bucklin), p. 5
(Christos Georghiou), p. 6 top (Kathy Gold), p. 8 (Linda Bucklin), p. 9 top (Sergei Bachlakov),
p. 9 bottom (Pius Lee), p. 11 (Fiona Ayerst), p. 13 top (Wampa & Ralf Juergen Kraft), p.
15 (Wampa), p. 16 top (DM7), p. 17 top (Kathy Gold), p. 17 bottom (Linda Bucklin), p. 20
(Bliznetsov), p. 27 (Andreas Meyer & Straga), p. 28 (Ozja), p. 29 bottom (Daniel Gale &
Cathy Keifer); WikiMediaCommons: p. 10, p. 13 bottom.
Cover: Shutterstock (DM7 & Unholy Vault Designs).

PO1434 / 2-2012

9 8 7 6 5 4 3 2 1

CONTENTS

All words in **bold** appear in the glossary on page 30.

MONSTERS!

Have you ever met a monster? Do you ever think there is one under your bed or hiding in your closet? It's unlikely because monsters are **imaginary creatures.**

Most monsters have an amazing feature, such as great strength. Some can breathe fire, while others may have two heads.

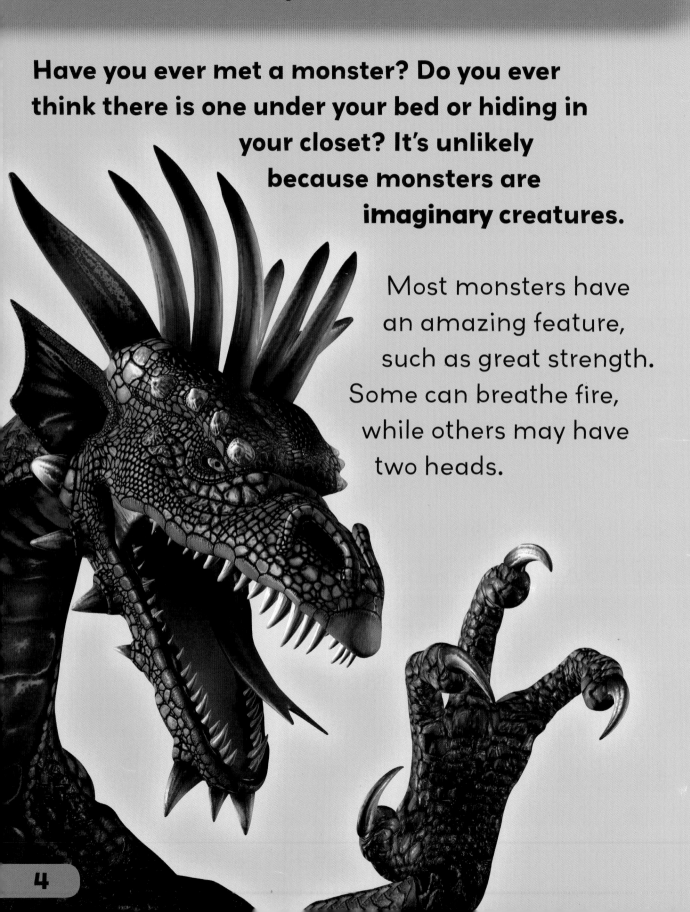

Many monsters come from old stories called **myths** and **legends**. These stories have been passed down over many years by storytellers.

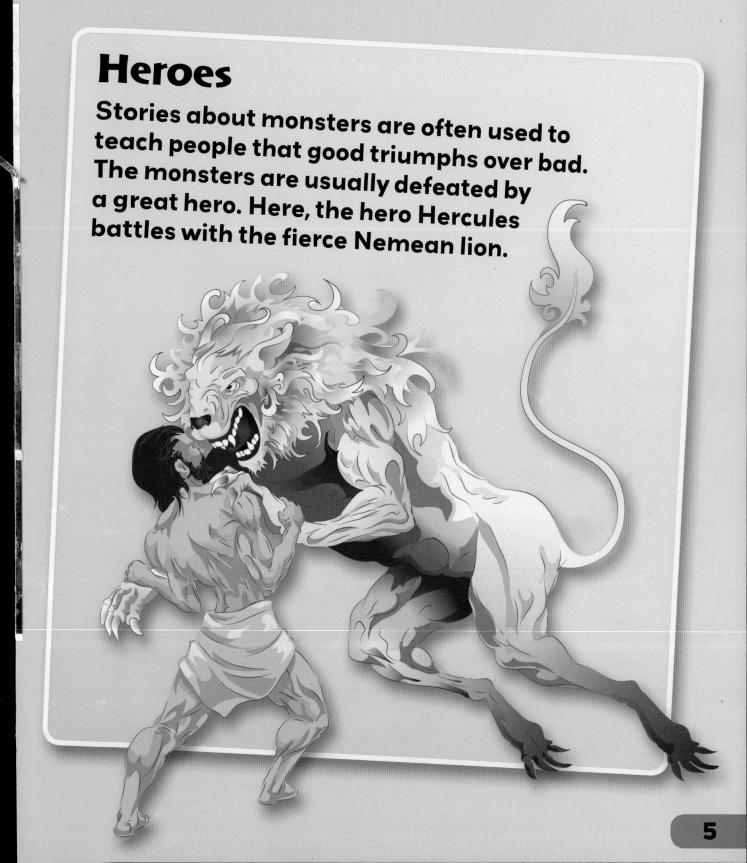

Heroes

Stories about monsters are often used to teach people that good triumphs over bad. The monsters are usually defeated by a great hero. Here, the hero Hercules battles with the fierce Nemean lion.

MYTHICAL MONSTERS

Monster tales began long ago in ancient times. People would tell stories about terrifying creatures that they hoped never to meet!

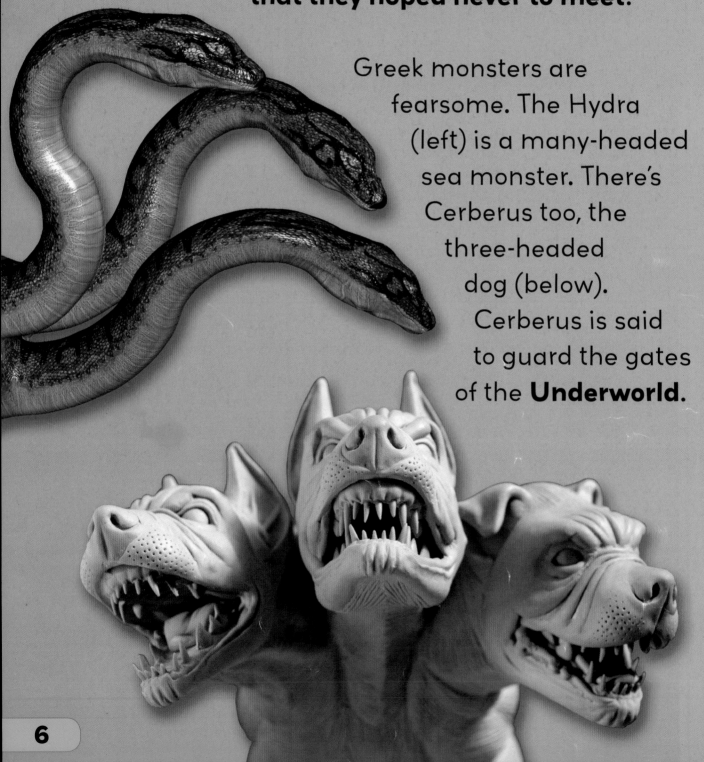

Greek monsters are fearsome. The Hydra (left) is a many-headed sea monster. There's Cerberus too, the three-headed dog (below). Cerberus is said to guard the gates of the **Underworld**.

Norse monsters are just as terrifying. Fenrir is a huge, fierce wolf. In stories, the gods chain him up but he breaks free.

IT'S AMAZING!

The Chimera is a horrifying Greek monster. It has the body of a lion, a tail that ends in a snake's head and the head of a goat on its back! Luckily, the mythical hero Bellerophon was able to defeat it with the help of Pegasus the winged horse.

DANGEROUS DRAGONS

You have probably read about dragons in stories and fairytales.

Traditional dragons are terrifying flying monsters. They have enormous leathery wings, tough scales, and clawed feet. Worst of all, they can breathe fire.

In China, the dragon is not a fearsome monster but a **symbol** of power, strength, and good luck. At festivals, people dress as dragons and parade through the streets.

Real-Life Dragons

Komodo dragons are the world's largest living lizards. They can be up to 10 feet (3 m) long. Komodo dragons are good hunters and can eat animals much bigger than themselves!

SEA MONSTERS

Oceans are very wide and deep. They are the perfect place for enormous monsters to hide!

The kraken is a giant squid that lives in the depths of the ocean. It comes from Norwegian **folklore**. In stories, the kraken drags ships below the water and feeds on the sailors.

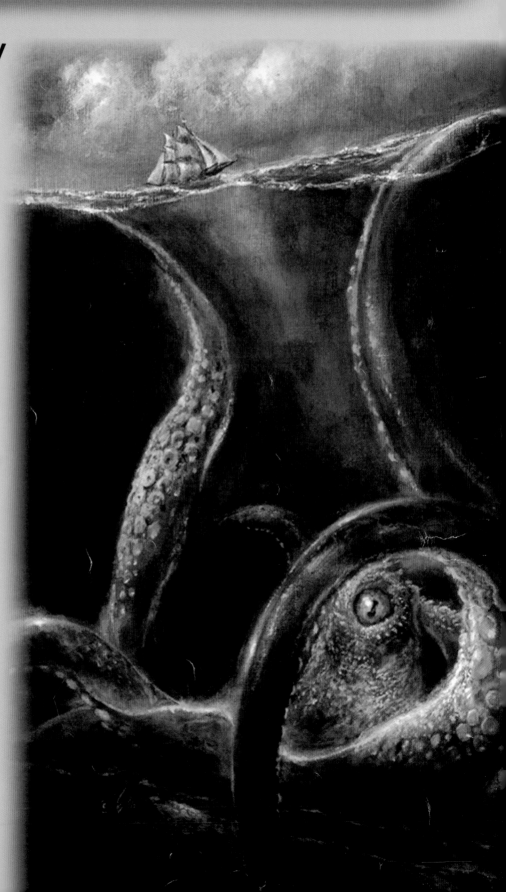

Real-life monsters live in the sea, too. Sharks are some of the scariest, though few will actually harm you. There are lots of different types of sharks.

This is a great white shark. It is one of the largest and deadliest of all the sharks.

IT'S AMAZING!

The whale shark is the biggest fish in the world. It has more than 4,000 teeth, but it uses them to capture tiny fish to eat. It is a gentle giant.

MONSTER REPTILES

Reptiles, such as snakes and lizards, can be scary enough. But imagine if they were fifty times bigger and had special powers!

The basilisk (above) is an ancient mythical creature. It is the king of the **serpents** and can kill a person or animal with a single glance.

There are other mythical creatures that are similar to the basilisk. The wyvern (below) has a dragon's head and the tail of a snake.

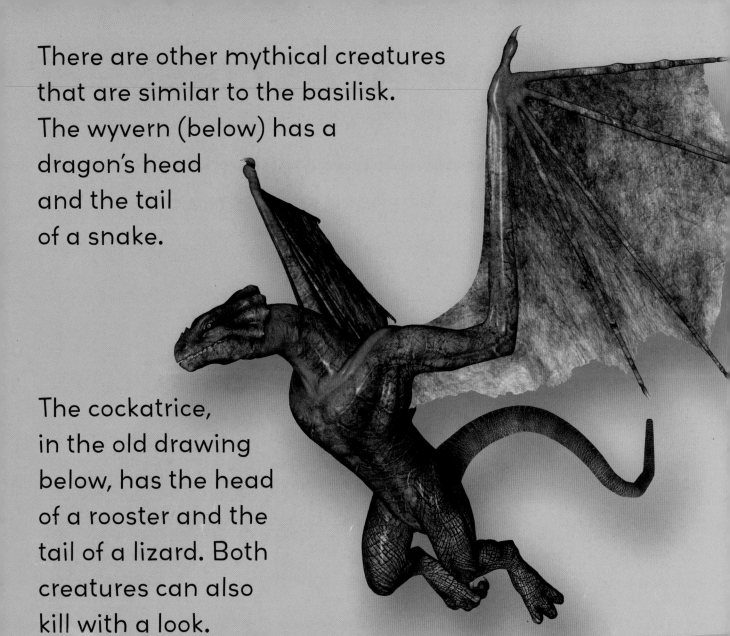

The cockatrice, in the old drawing below, has the head of a rooster and the tail of a lizard. Both creatures can also kill with a look.

Boy vs. Serpent

In *Harry Potter and the Chamber of Secrets*, young wizard Harry fights an enormous basilisk that has been hiding in Hogwarts School for many years.

13

MASHED-UP MONSTERS

Many mythical monsters are combinations of different animals. We have seen some of them already.

A griffin (above) has the head and wings of an eagle and the tail and body of a lion. The eagle is king of the birds and the lion is king of the beasts, so the griffin is a very powerful creature.

Centaurs are violent and **unruly** creatures that appear in Greek and Roman myths. They have the chest and head of a human, and the body and legs of a horse.

Centaur Chiron

In Narnia, a land created by author C. S. Lewis, centaurs are more gentle creatures. They are based on the mythical centaur Chiron, who was noble, wise, and powerful.

OGRES, TROLLS, AND GIANTS

Some monsters look like enormous or misshapen humans.

Ogres (right) are ugly, huge, and strong. They are also usually very unfriendly.

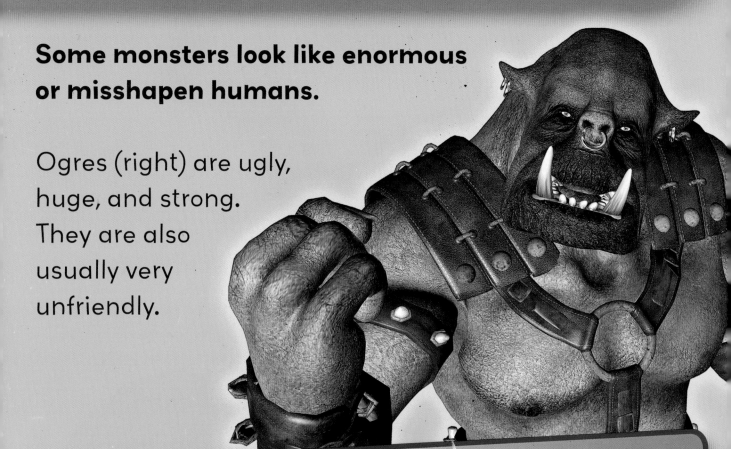

Shrek

The *Shrek* movies feature a different sort of ogre. Although Shrek is grumpy, he is also funny, loving, and very loyal to his friends.

Trolls (right) are ugly and mean creatures, and they are also a bit stupid. They live in caves, eat people, and sometimes even steal babies. In Scandinavian folklore, trolls turned to stone in sunlight!

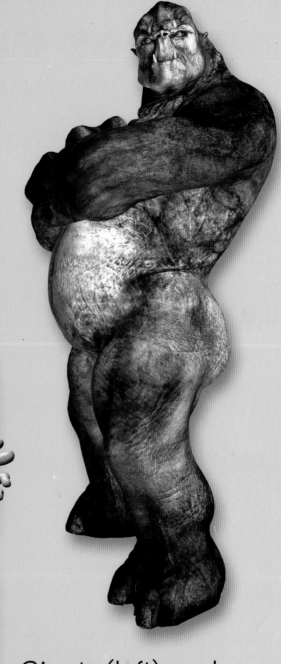

Giants (left) are huge, human-like creatures that are much bigger than us. Some are so strong that they can crush humans in their hands!

MAN-MADE MONSTERS

In some stories, monsters are created by people.

In a novel by Mary Shelley, a scientist named Victor Frankenstein creates a new man from the bones and body parts of dead people. Then he brings the monster to life with a bolt of lightning!

Frankenstein's Monster
The movie *Frankenstein* was made in 1931. It is considered one of the best horror movies of all time.

The golem (below) is another man-made monster. It comes from traditional Jewish stories.

A golem is a creature made from mud that is brought to life by a human. The golem serves the person who creates it.

SCARY MONSTERS

Monsters can be very scary. So, take a deep breath and count to ten before reading these pages!

Vampires are creepy creatures. Traditionally, they live forever, drink blood, sleep in coffins, cannot stand daylight, and can only be killed with a wooden **stake** through the heart.

Changing Vampires

In the *Twilight* series, author Stephenie Meyer has changed the traditional idea of vampires. The Cullen family of vampires protect humans, do not drink human blood, never sleep, and shimmer like diamonds in sunlight.

Zombies (right) are monsters that were once people. They are dead bodies that have come back to life. Zombies feast on human brains!

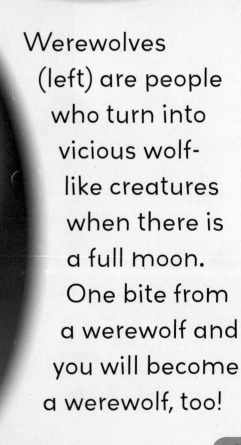

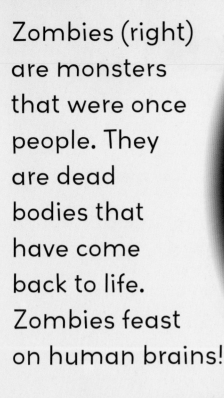

Werewolves (left) are people who turn into vicious wolf-like creatures when there is a full moon. One bite from a werewolf and you will become a werewolf, too!

MONSTERS IN MOVIES

Some of the most fantastic monsters appear in movies.

King Kong is a giant gorilla. He is captured and taken to New York. He escapes and crashes through the city!

Not So Bad!

In the movie *Monsters, Inc.*, monsters scare children and use the screams to power their city. When a little girl, Boo, gets into the monster world, the monsters discover that laughter is much more powerful than screams. From then on they make children laugh instead!

More amazing monsters were brought to life in the film versions of *The Lord of the Rings* novels. Shelob is an ancient spider-like monster that feeds on **orcs**. The Balrog hides deep below the Misty Mountains and is a fearsome creature made of shadow and fire.

ALIEN MONSTERS

No one knows what might live beyond planet Earth in outer space. People use movies to imagine what alien monsters might be like.

Gallaxhar (right) is a powerful alien commander in the movie *Monsters vs. Aliens*. He wants to replace all of the humans on Earth with **clones** of himself!

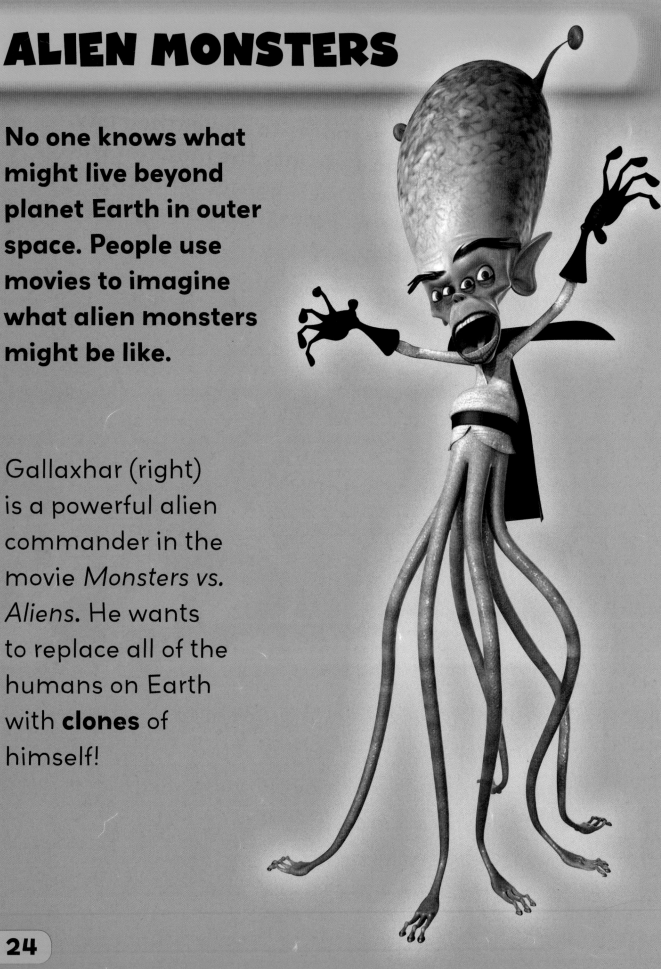

Aliens on Earth!

The *Men in Black* movies (below) starring Will Smith feature lots of scary-looking and unusual aliens. The Men in Black are agents that control aliens on Earth. Crazy creatures are a part of their everyday lives!

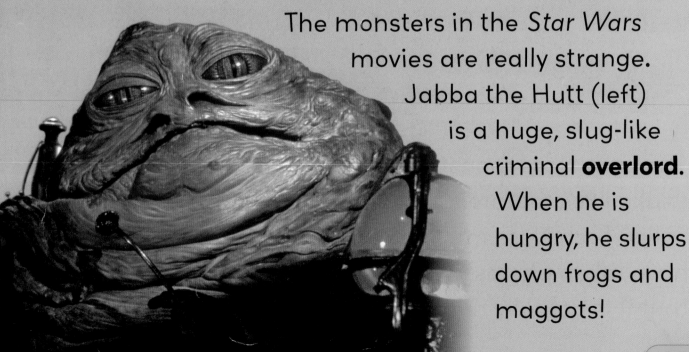

The monsters in the *Star Wars* movies are really strange. Jabba the Hutt (left) is a huge, slug-like criminal **overlord**. When he is hungry, he slurps down frogs and maggots!

REAL MONSTERS?

Many people around the world think that some monsters are real. They even say that they have seen or found evidence of them!

The Loch Ness monster is an enormous snake-like creature said to live in a giant lake called Loch Ness in Scotland. People claim to have taken photos of it, but no one can prove that it is actually real.

Bigfoot (right), also known as Sasquatch, is said to live in the Pacific Northwest region of the United States. Bigfoot is a huge, ape-like monster that walks on two legs and is covered in hair.

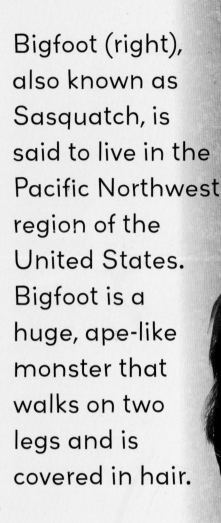

Finding Monsters

People have set out on expeditions to find bigfoot. Some claim to have found footprints, but none have found the actual beasts.

NATURE'S MONSTERS

Some of the most monstrous creatures live, or have lived, on the same planet as us.

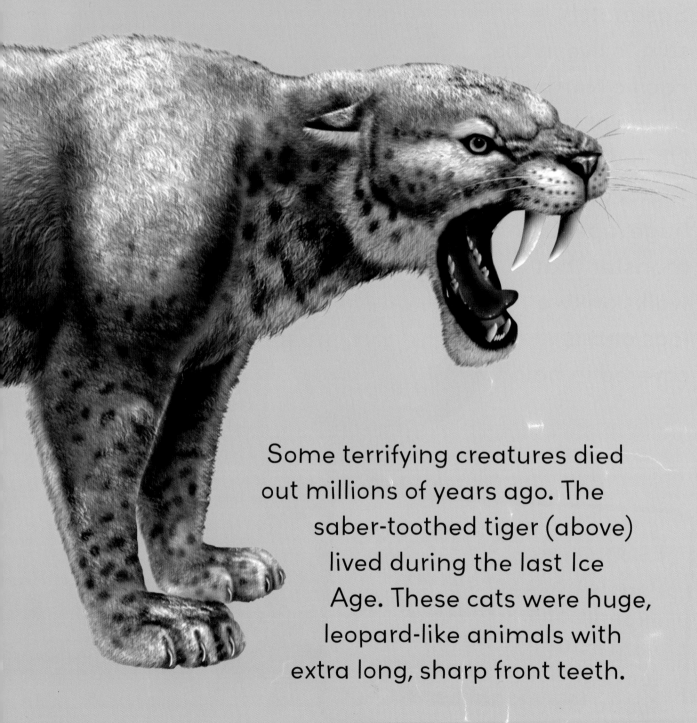

Some terrifying creatures died out millions of years ago. The saber-toothed tiger (above) lived during the last Ice Age. These cats were huge, leopard-like animals with extra long, sharp front teeth.

The angler fish (right) lives deep in the ocean and looks like something from a science-fiction movie. It attracts prey using a piece of **luminous** skin that dangles in front of its mouth. As soon as a creature gets too close, it strikes with its large, sharp teeth!

IT'S AMAZING!

The Venus flytrap plant snaps shut to trap insects that crawl onto it. It then eats the insects. Thank goodness these plants are very small!

GLOSSARY

clone an exact copy

evidence something that proves something is true

folklore stories and tales from a group of people in a country

imaginary something that is created by the imagination

legend a story that has been handed down from person to person through time

luminous glowing or giving off light

myth a story that comes from a particular tradition, handed down through time

Norse from ancient Scandinavia

orc a fierce human-like creature

overlord a ruler over other people

serpent a snake

stake a sharp, pointed piece of wood

symbol an object or picture that represents something else

Underworld an imaginary world beneath the Earth's surface where spirits live

unruly wild and hard to control

FURTHER INFORMATION

Books

Drawing Legendary Monsters series, Steve Beaumont, PowerKids Press, 2011.

Tracking Sea Monsters, Bigfoot, and Other Legendary Beasts, (Unexplained Phenomena), Nel Yomtov, Velocity, 2011.

Monsters, (Bookworms Chapter Books: For Real?), Dana Meachen Rau, Marshall Cavendish Benchmark, 2011.

Websites

Find out about some amazing creatures we share the planet with.
crazycreatures.org/

Find out about prehistoric monsters, and watch the National Geographic movie *Sea Monsters*.
www.nationalgeographic.com/seamonsters/kids/

The San Diego Zoo website contains lots of information about komodo dragons.
www.sandiegozoo.org/animalbytes/t-komodo.html

Find out about lots of mythical creatures on the American Museum of Natural History website.
www.amnh.org/ology/?channel=mythiccreatures

Movies

Harry Potter and the Chamber of Secrets, Warner Bros. Pictures, 2002.

King Kong, Universal Pictures, 2005.

Lord of the Rings; The Fellowship of the Ring (2001), *The Two Towers* (2002), *The Return of the King* (2003), New Line Cinema.

Men in Black, Columbia Pictures/Sony Pictures Entertainment, 1997.

Men in Black II, Sony Pictures Entertainment, 2002.

Monsters, Inc., Disney · Pixar, 2001.

Monsters vs. Aliens, DreamWorks Distribution, 2009.

Star Wars; The Phantom Menace (1999), *Attack of the Clones* (2002), *Revenge of the Sith* (2005), 20th Century Fox.

Star Wars; A New Hope (1977), *The Empire Strikes Back* (1980), *Return of the Jedi* (1983), 20th Century Fox.

INDEX

Note to parents and teachers: Every effort has been made by the publishers to ensure that the websites on page 31 are suitable for children, that they are of the highest educational value, and that they contain no inappropriate or offensive material. However, because of the nature of the Internet, it is impossible to guarantee that the contents of these sites will not be altered. We strongly advise that Internet access is supervised by a responsible adult.